GW00858781

INSIDE THE MIND OF A GAMBLER

The Hidden Addiction and How to Stop

STEPHEN RENWICK

Order this book online at www.trafford.com
or email orders@trafford.com

Most Trafford titles are also available at major online book retailers.

Print information available on the last page.

ISBN: 978-1-4907-6502-0 (sc)
ISBN: 978-1-4907-6500-6 (hc)
ISBN: 978-1-4907-6501-3 (e)

Library of Congress Control Number: Pending

Trafford rev. 09/04/2015

 www.trafford.com

North America & international
toll-free: 1 888 232 4444 (USA & Canada)
fax: 812 355 4082

Contents

Foreword

Photo by John Clark

My name is Stephen Renwick and I am psychology tutor and author. I am particularly interested in the psychology of gambling addiction. I am the author of *Tennis Is Mental* and *Tennis Is Mental Too*.

In *Inside the mind of a gambler* I look at a case study of a compulsive gambler, Guy. The book explores in detail the psychological aspects of gambling and enters the gambler's mind. There are many patterns of behaviour and mental processes common amongst the majority of pathological gamblers. After spending many hours interviewing Guy on his gambling addiction and how he thinks, I used the information to form the basis of this book. My aim is to help other gamblers with their addiction and ultimately to cease gambling. As a unique case study the book can also be used by psychologists and psychiatrists along with those interested in gambling addiction or psychology.

STEPHEN RENWICK

Dr Henrietta Bowden-Jones

As a clinician who has spent many years treating pathological gamblers, I found 'Inside the mind of a gambler' to be an honest and moving book describing the negative impact of problem gambling on the individual but also giving hope to readers about the availability and effectiveness of treatment.
Well done to Stephen Renwick, I will make sure our patients at the National Problem Gambling Clinic have the opportunity of reading his book.

Dr Henrietta Bowden-Jones
FRCPsych, BA(Hons), DOccMed, MD(Imperial)
Director and Lead Clinician, National Problem Gambling Clinic, London.
CNWL NHS Foundation Trust
Royal College of Psychiatrists Spokesperson on Behavioural Addictions.

Introduction

There are many forms of gambling and some are more popular than others. Betting shop machines, for example, offer a multitude of different games to play such as *Roulette, Rainbow Riches* and *Deal or No Deal* are just some of them. In Britain's betting shops there are about 8,700 shops and these have invested 2 billion into the local economy (www.gov.uk and the Association of British Bookmakers 2013). There are also approximately 32,000 machines making about £1 billion a year. One report found that Brits are blowing 1.7 billion per year on fixed odd machines (This is money, Sarah Bridge 2015) and in the UK there are about 28 million people who have participated in gambling over the past year (Health survey for England, 2012). This equates to 68% of men and 61% of women who gambled during this period.

The minimum stake for most of these games is £1 and the maximum pay-out on a single spin is £500. The odds of winning are fixed and it is easy to lose a lot of money when playing these types of games.

Gambling, unlike other addictions, has no apparent outward sign. Smokers hold cigarettes, drinkers clasp cans, drug users leave marks but gamblers are more difficult to spot. They are extremely good at hiding their problems and will go to extraordinary lengths to satisfy their gambling need.

This books looks at a specific case study of a pathological gambler, Guy. It shows how he fell into gambling, ruined his life, quit and then turned his life around. If you're a problem gambler then this book will give you some simple steps and strategies to help you quit.

Guy (not his real name) who was a gambler for around 20 years, has spent over £100,000, been bankrupt, suicidal and recovered. He now runs his own very successful business and no longer gambles. He wants to share his knowledge and experiences to help other people to quit their gambling addiction. Like any addiction, a gambling habit is not easy to break. However, with a few simple tools and skills that the author, Dr Henrietta Bowden-Jones and Guy offer, this book can help you on the road to recovery.

The first step is that you have to take a good hard look at yourself, be honest and admit you've got a problem. If you can't do that put this book back on the shelf and carry on gambling because it will eventually ruin your life. If you can be honest with yourself and face the facts then you've made the first step to becoming gambling free. I hope you enjoy reading my book and that it helps you with your gambling addiction.

PART 1

GUY

Chapter 1

Guy is in his early 40's and works as a sports coach, has never married and has no children. He has gambled for over 20 years.

Guy describes his early days and what got him into gambling.

In my teens I won £100 on a scratch card and this felt brilliant as back then it was a lot of money to me. I also watched my brother betting on horses with his mates and talking about them. Maybe this started me off on a road to becoming a compulsive gambler.

'In my early 20s I started to work down South as a sports coach. At the end of the day, in the club where I worked, I'd have a drink and play on the fruit machines. On one of machines the jackpot was £500. At the time that was a lot of money to win. I'd play on these machines for hours, sometimes putting all my wages into it.

This was the start of my gambling problem. I liked the buzz of winning and hated losing, just as when I was competing in my chosen sport. If the machine paid out I felt like a winner, but if it didn't I was desolate. I had to win at all costs.

Looking back I must have pumped thousands of pounds into these machines. After working at this particular club I started a job at different extremely prestigious London club. It didn't have any fruit machines, however a colleague of mine talked about how he'd won on roulette across the road. I had never been into a betting shop but I went with him once and put a couple of bets on roulette. My friend always bet on 0 and 2. He seemed to be winning so I copied him. I remember winning a few times and leaving with more money than I had when I went in. I thought, this is easy. I can make money doing this.

As time went on my friend and I would spend most days in the bookies across the road. We started to gamble a lot. My friend also went to casinos but I never really liked them. At the club where I was working I met a girl called Diana and immediately fell in love with her. It was literally love at first sight and we started dating. Our relationship became serious and we were inseparable. She came from an affluent background and I felt like I need a lot of money to fit in, therefore winning money would help me with this goal.

I was losing a lot of money gambling and ended up with about £40,000 of unsecured debts. Diana had no idea of this or my gambling habit. I used to tell her about my friend's gambling but made out it was him rather than me who had a problem.

Diana wanted to get married and have children. I wanted that too, but the problem was this dark cloud of debt over my head. It was getting even bigger. My gambling was getting worse and I felt the strain of not being able to give Diana what she wanted. I felt as if I wasn't good enough or I couldn't provide the lifestyle she wanted. After about 8 years into the relationship my debts were so big that I was struggling to pay them. I had to tell her I was in financial trouble. I knew this would possibly end the relationship but I also thought we loved each other and could make it work.

When I actually told her we were both very distressed. She asked me how I managed to get in to so much debt. I explained it was the expense of living in London. I couldn't get any more bank loans or credit cards. My big win hadn't come in either. I was finished. It's a feeling of despair, desperation and doom. It feels like having your heart ripped out and being completely helpless because there's nothing you can do about it and after all who would want a man with massive debts.

At home one evening I went to sleep only to wake up about 3 a.m. in a cold sweat. I was mentally working out what I owed. How could I ever pay it back? There was no way I could keep working and pay it back. It was just too much money. I fell back to sleep and when I awoke in the morning I checked how much money I had in my Halloween bowl. That's where I used to keep my loose change. I didn't have enough to buy a pack of crisps. It was diabolical. What should I do? Kill myself? Go bust? Something had to change quickly. I couldn't stay in London with no money.

I decided to go to the Citizens Advice Bureau in my local town. We sat down and worked out what I owed and what I could do about it. I had about 6 credit cards all maxed out, two or three loans and an overdraft. This was the worst financial mess id ever been in. I remember thinking I can't pay this back. The route I was advised to take was either bankruptcy or an individual voluntary arrangement, an IVA. I never thought I could own a home (even in the future) so I chose to enter into an IVA.

I had to pay back a proportion of the debt over 5 years. Even though I had to pay something back, at least it would be a fresh start. I chose to move back to my parents and save paying rent in London. Diana and I maintained our relationship for about 2 years but due to the distance, it gradually broke down. I couldn't give her what she wanted. I felt a complete failure. Most people have a wife and family. I had neither. I was such a loser. Gambling had ruined my life, my girlfriend's and our relationship.

I had to confess to my parents that I was going into an IVA and explain how I got into so much debt. Again, I said that it was the expense of living in London. I couldn't tell them I had a gambling problem as they would have been completely devastated. They couldn't have helped me either. I had to lie. To this day they still have no idea.

At the Citizens Advice Bureau they told me I would be unable to get any credit for six years and would be black listed. This meant there was no possible way to get into more debt and gamble. I had to start rebuilding my life from the bottom. I considered killing myself. But that seemed a coward's way out.

I had to face myself and deal with the mess I'd created. I was always good at finding solutions in life and taking positives from negatives. I thought, right, I have six years of hell so what can I do. When I was younger I always dreamt of gaining a degree, so I embarked on a distance learning degree with the Open University. This would keep me busy while I was in the IVA. Needless to say I graduated and paid back the IVA. It was now a clean start.

My relationship with Diana had broken down. I'd lost my job and entered into an IVA. It couldn't get any worse. I was in my late 20s living with my parents – how sad was that, I thought. It was very difficult to face the reality of my relationship breaking down and because I hate losing it was even harder to accept. I remember thinking, at least I don't have to see her face every day which would cause emotional heartache. I had to just get on with my life and put it down to experience.

A few years later I met a new lady, Claire who I love dearly. She was older than me, very wealthy and actually paid off half of my IVA. My mother paid the other half. I couldn't believe it and was so grateful to them. I just needed a break, a fresh start. That's what

I now had. I was so lucky to have met Claire and without her God knows where I would be. Homeless or dead most probably. She is my rock and is always there for me and someone who I never want to hurt.

Chapter 2

Guy describes a typical day in the life of a compulsive gambler

When I woke up in the morning I'd think about how I was feeling whether I had the urge to gamble or if I felt lucky. I would then run through possible winning outcomes and think about previous times when my ship had come in. Sometimes to enhance the feeling I'd play ocean 13 soundtrack to create more excitement about going to the bookies. This may sound odd but it helped to improve my confidence as a gambler. Next, I had to pick somewhere to go where I wasn't trying to avoid or excluded from. This might have involved some travel. I also considered how much I was willing to blow on that day which was typically £250-£750.

When I arrived I looked at the screens for any virtual races. These could pay well if you won on a combination or straight tri-cast. Indeed several years ago I won £5000 this way from a £2 stake on a straight tri-cast. If there were no races that took my fancy then I'd go and study the machines. I'd check roulette and deal or no deal for signs of pay-outs. If, for example, a deal or no deal red box was in the last few spins it could come again. If there were no red boxes then maybe it was due to come up. The same goes for roulette. If the numbers 0 or 2 had already come up I'd pick a different machine.

Another way of picking numbers was through external signs. When I looked at the clock in my car it was always 11:11. This happened lots of times. Was this a sign I'd win on the 49s with 11, 17, and 21? I thought I kept seeing 11 everywhere, that it was a sign from above or something, so maybe I'd pick it. When I finally played the machines, if there was no one else there, I'd play all 4 machines

INSIDE THE MIND OF A GAMBLER

at the same time. The hope here was that the computer might pick the same number on all machines and perhaps it's the number I've maxed out.

I took more chances now with gambling than in previous years. I was always thinking about how I could win more with one spin. That's why I played 4 machines, not just one. Although this costs 4 times the amount, there was the potential to win 4 times as much. So far I've only ever had two machines come in at the same time.

With this strategy I set a limit of £200. If I didn't win anything I'd more than likely go again with the same spins for another £200. This then meant I had to win the big pay-out in order to just break even or be £100 up. If all this failed it would add stress to my life and send me on a downer for a few days. I bounced back from this by changing bookies when I visited them or by going back to try and beat the machine that had just taken all my money.

I knew it was a stupid way of spending money and wasting it but it was an addiction. Once I started it was very hard just to walk away. All the time I saw people losing their money, popping out to the cash point and returning to the same machine on which they'd just lost. While they were at the cashpoint I would jump on their machine and do one spin to see if it paid. Sometimes id win and cash in before they even came back.

On the one hand they were chasing their losses and on the other trying to master the machine, or at least not feel beaten by it. The mind-set they had was 'surely it must pay now, I've just pumped loads into it.' If it didn't pay that day, they'd be back the next for a fresh start, hoping to catch the machine in a better mood.

Gamblers often treat these machines like living things, which have a mind or emotions. After my 4 machine spin strategy (which I called the 2k spin because if they all come in I'd win about £2000), I'd go home to reflect and rationalise my losses. This thought process allowed me to get rid of the feeling of guilt and depression by simply excusing my own behaviour.

Before leaving the bookies I would more than likely try my luck on the lotteries or horses just so I had something in the bank to look forward to. I'd then have the pleasure of checking the numbers in the evening or the next morning for the New York Lotto along with protecting the tickets in my wallet. Without these I wouldn't have been getting anything.

When I used to be a compulsive gambler this was my typical day. One key reason I used to gamble so much was boredom, too much time to kill, with the dream of winning big and doing what I pleased all day. I wanted the nice things without working myself to the bone. Gambling gave me that option.

One big error gamblers often make is when they win a large amount, for example £5000 or £10000. They'll go back and spend this trying to win bigger. They may increase their stakes, take bigger risks or show off in the bookies by waging maximum bets on each machine (spinning all the machines at the same time). This gives them the illusion that the machine recognises a serious player and is more likely to pay out big or the belief that all the machines are linked and they might produce the same number (which sometimes happened).

The key to wise gambling is to spend winnings wisely. Invest or buy something you can't gamble with. This will prevent you from spiralling back down and chasing your losses. If a gambler wins £5000 then loses it all, they would sink even lower into depression than before they had it. What they are trying to get is the winning feeling again, the dopamine rush or the elation of beating the machines. At the end of the day the bookies will always win because you'll go back again even after a win. You win, you spend and you lose.

I had a friend in London who won £12,000 one night in the casino playing roulette. Several days later when I asked him if he'd bought a car with the money he told me he went back to win more and lost it all. This was crazy. The chance of winning that amount is so slim. To get that sum of money and not do anything worthwhile with it is complete madness. But in the gambler's mind they are looking for the same fix again. They'll spend everything they have and more to get it. This is when you know you're a compulsive gambler and need help. It's almost as though winning any amount would not be enough.

When I had a decent win, I chose to use it for property renovation and a house deposit. This made more sense as I figured it's not every day I'll win this type of money and it's even harder to save. It therefore made sense to invest rather than put back. After one win for example I bought a Rolex watch just so I wouldn't blow the winnings again. It was a nice Rolex that I didn't need but it saved me spending it on roulette.

I've never really liked casinos even though the owners try to make them attractive - free meals, drinks and pretty women spinning the roulette wheels. I always preferred the small bookies. There you could do what you wanted. Play every machine, if you felt like it. I think it's a control thing where I felt more comfortable, dictating how I gambled. I also enjoyed people seeing me spin all four machines at once and watching them look at the four roulette tables to see what number came up. I would of course spin around in my traditional semi-circle for good luck. Another thing I would do is to pull the chairs back to create space between the chairs and the machines. This allowed me to walk around. These are classic rituals that I learned along the way through conditioning.

If I lost on everything, I'd buy the national lottery tickets just as a backup. I never really liked buying these as the odds are ridiculous. However, I did discover what's called 'Hot picks' which pays 450-1. I would place 5 rows of three numbers (all the same) in order to win £2,250. I never won any of these bets. It actually felt like as if I was saving money here. I spent £100s in the bookies and £20 with the national lottery tickets. That's how the pathological gambler thinks.

Chapter 3

An interview with Guy by Stephen Renwick

Why did you gamble Guy?

I'd been gambling for that long that I didn't even know why I was doing it. It became a big part of my daily life. I thought I was gambling to win money but even if I won I ended up going back and losing the winnings only to chase them again. It doesn't make sense. It was a massive urge to gamble it back.

I think one reason I gambled is that it gave me a rush and was a huge thrill, especially when I was winning. I hated losing. I'm highly competitive and will do almost anything to come out on top. I had to beat the machine. I'd tried to quit but always ended up going back again. I knew I needed to stop but the urges were so strong it was very difficult. I believed I would one day hit the big win and would never have to work or gamble again.

Gambling helped me escape my anxiety and depression. I felt I hadn't made the most of my life. I dreamt of being married with a happy family, kids and nice home etc. But things didn't turn out that way. I felt trapped and that I needed a lot of money just to get by. Winning money from gambling would have made life easier.

I had a couple of decent wins but I spent that money. I wanted to feel a success. People tend to judge you by how much money you have. I therefore figured if I could win a lot then I would be accepted and liked by others. I know that I had low self-esteem that I wasn't worth much. That's why I had to spend the winnings on gambling again and I felt that I wasn't worthy of having money. I thought gambling was my way of dealing with other problems because It distracted me from not being happy at work, having no life goals, that I wasn't married, with no children.

Later on in life I tragically lost my older brother due to an undiagnosed heart problem and then one year later I lost my father to cancer. This was a sad time and very stressful. At this point I realised that we can't take anything with us and gambling will not give me the miracle life I was looking for, if anything it would make it worse.

Did you enjoy gambling?

I loved it and hated it. I loved the thrill and excitement of putting money on a number and then spinning the wheel. There was no better feeling than waiting for the wheel to spin and the ball landing on my number. I'd played the game so long I knew if I'd won from the position of the ball and how the wheel started. You get to know the pattern of the spin and the angle the ball will go into the numbers and then roughly where it's going to land.

On the other hand I hated it as it cost me a lot of money, especially when I was down, chasing my losses. Winning was a fantastic feeling but losing very stressful. In my mind I would be calculating my month's wages, how much more I could afford to lose and things like that. If I had a couple of bad weeks when I was losing and financially struggling, I did sometimes think about ending my own life. It would have been a permanent escape from the problem. I admit I did think about it. Gambling is an addiction, an illness and it can get out of hand pretty quickly.

Do people know you're a former addicted gambler?

A couple of my close mates do and they don't really speak to anyone else. My mother has no idea and would probably kill me if she knew. It's something that I really struggle with as I've always tried to solve my own problems. I used gambling as an escape. If I won I'd be quite generous but if I lost I just got depressed and frustrated. My girlfriend didn't really know the extent of my problem. She just thought I bet every now and again. I wouldn't tell her that I had a major problem with it because I didn't want to upset her.

I attended a Gamblers Anonymous meeting years ago but didn't really like it. One man in there looked like he'd lost everything and had even sold his kids' toys to fund gambling. Terrible. You really saw the destruction it can do to people. That's why I would rather ring Gam Care which actually helped me quit. They're great because they understand how you think as a gambler and what questions to ask you, which enable you to avoid betting.

The interesting thing is that none of my family were gamblers apart from my brother who used to bet on horses. He wasn't a pathological gambler but I remember him betting and waving the slips around. I used to look up to him so maybe this is where I got it from. Overall, some close friends know about my gambling problem, but my immediate family doesn't. I'm good at hiding it from them and keeping it very low key.

Did you ever think about quitting when you were gambling?

I thought about quitting only when I started to lose a lot of money and get into debt. The problem is that you always think the big win will come in and you'll be able to clear all your financial problems. Of course, you're lucky if you win a decent amount. Most people don't.

When I was winning it was great and there was no point quitting as it gave me more money to bet with. I could go for higher bets and have the potential to win more. It's a catch 22. You win, you spend and you lose. What made me quit was having a quiet sit down and wondering where I was going in life and what impact gambling would have on my future. I really had to wake up and smell the coffee. Yes I had a few good wins but it was all too easy to put it all back again.

One time after I had a big win I thought this probably wouldn't happen again, so I used it for a house deposit. I wanted to have a complete break from the chains of gambling. I knew inside I had to make a massive change in my life style and set goals for the future. That's why I went round and resisted all the attractions of betting shops. I had to make it extremely difficult to place a bet. I bought internet blocking software so I couldn't access gambling sites. I opened a Santander business account where the card wouldn't work on gambling sites.

I started to change my route to work, cut up credit cards and began activities that would fill up my time. It really came down to what Gam Care had told me to control - time, money and location.

Once you get into a new routine it becomes your norm and you don't think about gambling all the time. You start to think, "I'll treat myself to lunch today." Better that, which costs about £20, than blowing £200 in 10 minutes on roulette. I realised I could have a better life style without gambling, that there are other ways to make money and it needn't happen overnight. There's more pride in doing it this way than gambling.

As a former compulsive gambler what advice would you give others who want to quit?

If you have a gambling addiction it's not easy to stop. There are no quick fixes. However, with the right strategy and mind-set you can resist the urge to gamble. I'd tried many times to quit only to fall back, ending up once again in the bookies playing roulette on the machines.

The difficulty I had was not funding the habit but controlling the urges and thoughts. If I was sitting at home and a TV advert came on such as Mr Green showing the roulette wheel spin, this would plant the seed for me to go and try my luck. For years I had the dilemma of wanting to quit but also wanting to gamble. I would sometimes go online to bet only to lose and then close the account as a way to avoid gambling again.

The problem is that there are hundreds of online casinos. Once you've closed one account it's easy to open another. Once I actually won about £3000 on online roulette and cashed in, only to spend it again in the betting shop. It's a cycle, you win, you spend and then you lose.

In the betting shops they now have a spending limit control where you can set a restriction on the money you gamble. If you're a compulsive gambler they're a waste of time as you can simply click on NO for setting a limit.

After numerous failed attempts to stop I called Gam Care, the gambling hotline. They offer anonymity. When you are feeling the urge to gamble they can really help. They get you to think differently, not act on impulse.

Another reason I stopped was by controlling time, location and money. If I didn't have loads of spare time, access to money or was not in the area of betting shops, I would be less likely to be tempted.

It did help to keep these factors in mind each day. I'd take a different route in the car or leave credit cards at home – just to break the pattern. Keeping busy all day was vital; anything to take my mind off gambling. I used to gamble a lot when I was really bored or had nothing else to do.

These three crucial factors: Time, Location and Money. All three helped me to stop gambling. CBT helped me question my belief system and alter my thought process and question my irrational beliefs. I had to change what I felt about gambling. I had to look at my life and think where I was going. What did I want? I needed to alter my thinking. I was worth more than what I was demonstrating, emotionally, physically and financially. I had to change. I had no other choice.

I had to learn to re-condition myself and to unlearn all the conditioning that had taken place over the years. For this I used mental imagery. I imagined something that I really hated - rats.

I imagined rats were outside and inside the shops and they were on the floor around the machines. I seriously hate rats. The thought of betting shops being infested with them put me off going in. I mentally rehearsed this picture. After several days I felt differently when I thought about the bookies.

I also used a more positive scenario of having saved £10,000. I tried to feel what this would be like. Rather than trying to get rich quick by gambling I had a new mind-set and some new goals. I also finally realised that after 20 years of wasting money I had to change paths. The current path could only end in self-sabotage, destruction and ultimately loss.

If you're reading this and thinking it sounds like you then surely it's time to change. It's far better to find enjoyment doing something else.

I imagined I was in a rocking chair at the end of my life, looking back. If I could see myself reviewing my life, thinking, my god all I've done is waste thousands of pounds and have nothing to show for it, no family, debts unpaid, then this would motivate me to change direction. After all I was making the choice to gamble each day. Well, at least I thought I was. There is not a history of addiction in my family. Did I want a life that was wasted? No. I had to beat this terrible addiction before it destroyed me.

The key is to be really honest with yourself. Most gamblers live in denial about their problem. You have to face the cold hard truth.

If you don't it will be too late. This doesn't mean you have to attend Gamblers Anonymous meetings. They are excellent but you may be quite a private person. Group therapy could put you off. Gam Care or The Samaritans are excellent alternatives, especially when you feel that urge to gamble. Outside help like that gives you time to think. You don't have to act immediately and it could ultimately save you a lot of money.

You have to take a look in the mirror, face the facts and the truth about your problem. Unless you can do this you'll still be gambling in the future. The key is to completely stop and withdraw from gambling, not just cut down (especially if you're a pathological gambler). This means total abstinence.

You also need to change the way you think and what you're focusing on. Try to switch your thoughts from winning money, boredom and quick fixes to life with a plan, with goals. Most gamblers have a short horizon. They don't care too much about 5 or 10 years down the line. The truth is that one day in 10 years you'll arrive somewhere, the question is where? Where do you want to be? Choose a new path, walk down a new street, realise there's more to life than gambling your money away and getting into debt. Be good to yourself and stop self-sabotaging. Don't see gambling as a way of earning money. It isn't. It a quick way of losing a lot of money.

Even when you do win I bet (excuse the pun) you go back and gamble it back thinking you can place higher bets to win more. It can't be money you want as when you get it you throw it away. It's rather a sense of excitement, achievement, filling an abyss of low self-esteem. The past has gone. You have to put that behind you and look forward to a future free from gambling. I remember reading somewhere about how you can't drive a car looking into the rear view mirror or you're going to crash. The same was true in life, you have to keep looking forward.

When you feel like gambling it really helps to keep a diary of your thoughts and how much you spend. This will then be telling evidence of the reality of your gambling problem. It might make you realise you're actually spending a lot more than you think.

I remember being in the bookies and going back and forth to the cash point. After about 20 minutes I thought I'd spent about £250. But when I checked my bank statements the truth was I'd lost £550. A diary also helps you question your beliefs and thoughts prior to betting.

Typical thought diary entry for Guy

Monday:

Initial thoughts: I've got 4 hours off this morning. I feel lucky. Might bet on lunchtime and teatime 49s. My limit today is £50.
What happened: Bet £50 on 49s and then started playing roulette. Thought to myself I'll try £100 on 3 machines. Lost the £100. Went back to cash point. Spent £40
Lost £400. Gutted. Feel stressed now. Chasing losses again. Hate myself.
Reality - spent £600 in one day. Won nothing. Felt down and depressed and quite stressed. Had to leave as started having a panic attack.
Next time I feel the urge to gamble I must question my belief. For example, say "there is a higher chance of me losing money today which will put me even further into debt.'
What else could I do today that is more productive and doesn't lose me a lot of money? Maybe I should count to 10 before acting on my impulse and plan a different activity. I could call Gamcare and talk about my urges.

Another method is to work on raising self-esteem. I felt I wasn't worth much and therefore didn't deserve money. I felt I had to get rid of it. This meant that even when I won I was compelled to spend it on gambling again. It wasn't really about winning money but more about one's self-worth. Therefore, if you increase your self-worth you'll feel less compelled to get rid of money that you have.

Sometimes gambling fills a gap in your life. It could be boredom, depression or stress. Working on other areas of your life can really help you stop gambling. You also have to realise that gambling won't make you less depressed or less anxious. Even a win would be short lived. The truth is, it will probably make them worse.

You would be better off joining a sports club, reading or pursuing some other interest. Fill your day with different activities. This helps you create some new positive habits rather than gambling, which is a destructive way of life.

The above examples should help you see how much you're spending and show you the evidence that you're actually losing more than you win. They could also help you to question your idea that you're winning and doing well at gambling. Writing down your thoughts should help you see how futile thinking like that is and how it's ruining your life.

Keep a diary for a couple of weeks and see the patterns that emerge. Then change your thoughts to something more helpful (See the CBT section).

You should also write down reasons for and against gambling so you can see them in front of you.

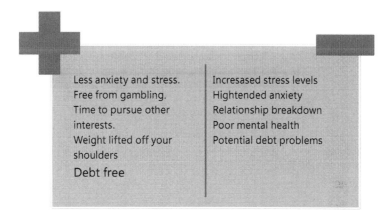

Less anxiety and stress.	Increased stress levels
Free from gambling.	Hightended anxiety
Time to pursue other interests.	Relationship breakdown
	Poor mental health
Weight lifted off your shoulders	Potential debt problems
Debt free	

Fig 2. Shows the benefits of stopping gambling and the negatives of carrying on.

Reasons why people gamble

- Stress
- Escape
- Boredom
- Distraction
- Motivated by past wins
- Problems relaxing
- OCD
- Rebellious
- Inherited genes
- Low self esteem
- Feeling like you've underachieved in life
- Wanting a quick life fix
- Fun winning
- Pay debts
- Delusional beliefs about winning
- Buzz

Reasons why Guy gambled

- Boredom
- Despression
- Chasing losses
- Escaping problems
- Feeling good at it

Fig 3. Different reasons why people might gamble

Chapter 4

Post interview reflection on Guy's gambling addiction by Stephen Renwick

Guy has lost about £100,000 mainly through betting shop gambling. He's had suicidal thoughts (especially after big losses) and has an anxiety or panic disorder. Gamblers think differently from other people. They process information in a different way.

Guy says it started when he was 16 and won £100 on a scratch card. Back then it was a lot of money. How then did he find himself years later gambling 1000s of pounds in the bookies, popping back and forth to the cash point and then ending up in financial ruins?

Guy gambled most days and mainly played roulette, 49s draw and deal or no-deal. The 49s draw is a twice daily draw where you can pick numbers 1- 49 and between 1-6 numbers. For example, you could pick three numbers 2, 5, 7 and win 600-1 or 349-1 (depending if it is the 6 or 7 ball draw).

Guy had problems controlling his impulses and found it difficult to stop gambling even when winning. Playing roulette, he regularly chased his losses. A typical day for Guy would be to spend anything from £100 - £1000 on the machines and dispose of a large proportion of his wages. Guy preferred local betting shops to online and casinos. Having played them for many years, he felt he knew the machines better.

Over a number of years Guy started to increase his stakes, trying to win bigger pay-outs. Guy did this by playing more than one machine at a time, hoping to increase the pay-out if he won. If the roulette machine paid out £496.80 then playing two machines would pay-out £993.60. If he played 4 machines and his numbers came up he could win £1987.20. Sometimes Guy would put the maximum stake on roulette which was £13.85 and hoped that all four machines land on the same number. In 20 years it never happened. The closest was winning on 2 out of 4 machines.

Guy bet on his favourite numbers 0 and 2. Before placing any bets on these machines Guy would look at the previous numbers drawn to decide if he was going to gamble. The criteria that needs to be met is quite interesting. On a roulette reel the numbers either side of 0 are 26 and 32 and either side of number 2 are 21 and 25. Therefore, if any of these numbers had come up, Guy would place a high bet in the belief that his number 0 and 2 were due.

The roulette machine is a fixed odds and random ball generator. Guy, however, like many gamblers, believed there was a pattern or higher chance of winning depending on the previous numbers drawn. Guy thought the way he behaved could also influence a machine. In some sense he regarded the machine as a human with feelings, thoughts and emotions.

Guy sometimes made irrational decisions and believed he had skills which could increase his chance of winning. For example, if the roulette machine was landing very close to either of his numbers, 0 or 2, he thought the machine was getting ready to pay out big. This therefore meant he should increase his stake and wait for the 'Jacky' as he calls it (meaning jackpot). Sometimes this tactic paid off and he won a large amount. More often than not, he ended up chasing his losses. He saw the money lost as an investment in that machine which he thought would pay out at a later date.

Like other gamblers, Guy also bet on lottery draws, the 49s and New York Lotto. The pay-out on these can be quite high. UK Roulette pays out 36-1 whereas the 49 draw is 600-1 and the New York lotto up to 1000-1 for three numbers on a six ball draw. So, if Guy placed a £10 bet on the New York lotto (six ball draw) and his three numbers came up he would win £10,000. There are also other cases where gamblers have used lucky numbers, for example:

There was a case when the Bet safe Caribbean Dream Cruise offered gamblers 60 thousand euros to the winner of the tournament. The winner was Tedh from Sweden who won the 60 thousand euros. On his hand (as a child) he had a burn mark that looked like the number 3 and this was his lucky number. He also had a bracelet with the number 3 on. The casino offered to double his winnings on red or black and Tedh gambled on red. He won and the roulette ball landed on, you guessed it, no.3. Was this luck or his lucky number?

Guy's gambling habits have gradually changed. To get the same excitement he now needed higher pay-outs. Again, he had set numbers that he used 2, 5, 7 or 11, 17, 21. Based on past wins and operant conditioning, these acted as Guy's lucky numbers.

Interestingly, Guy won £7500 on the 49s draw with the numbers 11-17-21 and he won £5000 on the New York lotto with the numbers 2-5-7. Of course Guy showed recall bias and would only tell you about his wins rather than his losses. Guy also remembers winning £5000 on a £2 stake using a straight tri-cast on handicapped horse races with the numbers 2-5-7. He used his lucky numbers for this race and didn't even look at the odds of each horse and amazingly won a significant amount of money.

Another time Guy recalled was when he visited the casino. He never really liked casinos but on this particular evening he felt the urge to explore. Once Guy had become a member he took around £1500 and bet on roulette numbers 0 and 2. In his mind he wanted to do £100 spins with £50 on each number and therefore winning £1800 if it came in.

Guy remembers playing some of the fruit machine games first, winning a couple of hundred pounds and then having dinner. As he was having dinner he kept a close eye on the roulette table numbers. He was waiting for 32, 26 or 21 and 25 to come up. This was his strategy through his entire gambling career. He thought that if 32 or 26 came up then soon it would be 0. If 21 or 25 came up then 2 must be there soon.

At first, Guy put £25 down on 2 to test the waters and he actually won. With his big pile of chips on the table and everyone watching he felt great. After about another 10 or so spins his chip pile was depleting and Guy changed tables. He started to bet higher stakes with the hope of hitting it big. He did several £100 spins with £50 on 0 and £50 on 2. They didn't come in.

Guy was left with about £250. In desperation he decided that he would go even bigger. He put £125 on each number, walked around in his classic lucky semi-circle and watched the ball go round. His number didn't come up. He was gutted. His first thought was he could have been £720 up and now he was down. Guy remembered going to the cash point only to realise it didn't accept his Santander business card. He was then trapped in the dilemma of quitting or going elsewhere to get some cash.

He actually went downstairs and closed his casino membership. After that he decided to stick to betting shops. His dream night of winning big and walking away with several thousand pounds had ended on a real negative. The casino dream hadn't worked out for Guy and he walked away a loser.

It is often said that the bookies always win. Why then do people like Guy carry on gambling?

We are constantly exposed to images of gambling - TV adverts, the internet or high street shops. For a majority of gamblers it is a habit that spirals out of control. Even when they know the odds are against them they still continue to gamble. The gambler is under the illusion that they are skilful enough to control the outcome.

Guy used the numbers on the previous roulette draws to determine when to put money on his lucky numbers 0 and If these had come up, he thought his chances would have been higher. A recipe for disaster is when this is combined with intermittent pay outs (operant conditioning schedule). It becomes an extremely difficult addiction to break.

In terms of ritualistic behaviours Guy believed that the best time to play was after 6pm when the machines have been pumped with cash all day. They were probably full and on the cycle of paying out. He thought that the machines went through cycles of input and output. He wanted to play them when they were paying out and believed that the machines were linked. This meant to Guy that if he plays all the machines at the same time then the same random ball generator would produce the same number on all machines.

This is based not on evidence but a gambling fallacy otherwise known as the Monte Carlo Fallacy. This basically suggests that if something happens more often than normal it will happen less in the future or vice versa. The problem for Guy and many gamblers was that even if they won they would inevitably return to try and win bigger amounts by pouring all their winnings into the same machine. The gambler would then try to rationalise this loss and need to win again to get the same buzz.

There is plenty of research into brain reward areas and receiving monetary wins, for example, the striatum is crucial for responding to natural reinforces such as food or sex (Dr. Clark, Wolfson Brain Imaging Centre). This could be used to explain why Guy chased his losses and was prepared to lose everything in order to win. In his mind he had to feel as if he had conquered the machine or mastered the game. This led him to play the machine for longer and try to win back any losses. Guy recalled when he was about £500 down and had to get another £300 to gamble on the same machine. He eventually ended up even after about 4 hours of trying to win big with his money back. This meant he had to win £800 to be even again. This psychological trap gets gamblers into real financial trouble.

When playing roulette Guy mentioned that if numbers very close to his selected numbers came up he would then bet for longer. Numbers 26, 32, 21 or 25 are close to 0 and 2. If any of them came up he would then stay on that machine with the belief that the machine would pay within 5 spins. These near misses act as a pointer that the gambler is mastering the game. They are under the illusion they can predict the numbers. In reality, they have no control over the machine and each number has an equal chance. If Guy could have actually put the ball into the spin he said he would have stayed even longer. This is a kind of variation of personal choice and would probably have led to higher bets.

Ritualistic behaviour is another way of showing how the gambler thinks he can influence the outcome. Guy talked about how he would press the roulette spin and then turn around in a semi-circle away from the machine and then back again. This made Guy feel like the next spin would be the winning spin. If he did win he would attribute it to the semi-circle turn. If he didn't win, he would think his turn wasn't correct or that he turned too fast.

He explained how he would do this on two or more machines with the aim of winning as much as £1000 or £1500. This was because he now had no interest in winning £100 or £200. If he did win these amounts he would simply use them to reinvest in more spins with the chances of winning big. Thus as time goes by the thrill of winning increases. Like a drug addiction, gamblers need more of it to get the same high.

PART 2

The Psychology of Gambling

Chapter 5

What are the signs that you may have a gambling problem?

These can be broken down into different areas including behavioural, physical, cognitive and psychosocial.

1: Behavioural: High frequency of gambling, betting higher amounts, chasing losses or lying about your gambling habits.

2: Physical: Anxious when betting, poor diet or physical and mental exhaustion after betting.

3: Cognitive: Obsessive thoughts about gambling or highly impulsive.

4: Psychosocial: Gambling as a means of dealing with your problems, feeling bad or guilty after gambling or even suicidal thinking.

Psychological and physiological processes gamblers go through prior, during and post gambling.

Prior to gambling

1: Fear of missing out if their number comes up
2: Preoccupied with thoughts of gambling
3: Strong urges and impulses about gambling

<u>During the act of gambling</u>

1: Physical arousal of the ANS – fight or flight
2: Superstitious and ritualistic behaviours
3: Irrational thoughts either internal or external

<u>Post gambling</u>

• If you won

1: Positive reinforcement
2: Supports the player's belief system
3: A sense of victory over the machines

• If you lost

1: Stress and anxiety at losing money
2: Anger at oneself.
3: Approach and avoidance thinking
4: The belief that the machines will pay and the money spent is rightly yours to get back

Risk Factors in Gambling

Stress

Some people gamble as a way of dealing with everyday stress or hassles. Sometimes individuals exposed to high stress levels such as Post Traumatic Stress Disorder are more vulnerable to addictions like gambling. A gambler can use betting as an escape from reality. A gambler could also have a secondary condition such as anxiety or depression. Gambling, although used as a distraction or avoidance, can sometimes increase anxiety or depressive episodes (especially after a loss).

Peers

Social identity theory suggests that the person adopts the group norms of other gamblers and the group they belong to. Positive reinforcement from peers will contribute to the operant conditioning process. If for example, someone wins £500 playing roulette, the player might get patted on the back by friends and praised for winning. This is what B.F. Skinner termed 'operant conditioning'. If behaviour is rewarded then it is more likely to be repeated. In gambling, a win is a reward. To get more rewards, more wins or near misses are needed. This means more gambling, which in turn means more spending.

Age and sex

Gamblers can be any age but young people may do it as a means of trying to pay bills or college fees. Gamblers are male or female. More females gamble than you may think. In the bookies Guy had noticed an increased number of women betting. Research by the Gambling Commission found that:

- *75% for men and 71% for women gamble*
- *Men were more likely than women to take part in most gambling activities*
- *Bingo was one exception (12% for women and 6% for men)*
- *Scratch cards (25% for women and 23% for men)*

Personality

Extroverts are normally under-aroused or bored. They want to experience a high to increase cortical arousal. They may have an addictive personality trait and have impulsive issues when gambling. Pathological gamblers may also be dependent on rewards. They learn to link one outcome with a behaviour e.g. winning on roulette and feeling excited. Completing a personality profile could help to identify your traits.

Genes

If your parents were gamblers this puts you at an increased risk of gambling addiction which shows a genetic link. Most pathological gamblers could have another condition alongside their gambling problem, such as anxiety or depression. This shows there is a chance of two conditions co-occurring. In terms of the environment, factors such as stress, peer pressure and even some medications can put you more at risk.

Some classic risk factors include:

- being male
- starting at an early age
- being highly competitive
- having another mental health concern

There is more than likely going to be an interaction between the environment and the gene (diathesis stress), which may suggest that stress could activate a specific gene.

Different types of gamblers.

After spending time researching gambling and talking to Guy it appears that there are different reasons why people gamble. Gamblers tend to fall into one of two categories; escape or action. Guy was an escape gambler, someone who bets alone and wants to escape from depressive feelings. Gambling acts as a numbing tool and allows the gambler to avoid other people. An action gambler gains pleasure from the thrill of being a gambler. Gambling is their drug equivalent and they are happy to gamble with others.

To see if a gambler has a clinical problem we have to look at the psychological criteria in the Diagnostic Statistical Manual (DSM 5). To be diagnosed with a gambling addiction some of these have are required:

1: Preoccupation with gambling
2: Lying
3: Loss of control
4: Chasing losses
5: Bailout
6: Tolerance
7: Escape
8: Risking relationships

Five or more of the above is a sign you are a pathological gambler

Guy appeared to use gambling to escape pain in other areas of his life such as work and relationships. He explained to me that he wasn't happy with his career anymore and wanted to win big so that he didn't have to be a slave to his job. He spent most of his wages in the bookies and each week lost a lot of money. He regularly chased his losses and sometimes dug himself into quite serious debt problems. This he kept to himself. His partner had no idea of the extent of Guy's gambling. Guy did a very good job of concealing his gambling addiction. In fact, he didn't admit to himself he had a problem. He was in denial about his habit and actually believed he had his gambling under control.

It wasn't until many years later and the bankruptcy IVA proceedings that Guy finally broke down and admitted he had a problem. He was on the road to recovery and attended many Gamblers Anonymous sessions. He avoided gambling opportunities and had no credit cards or loans to dip into.

Years later, after graduating, Guy now owns his first home and has a stable business and partner. He wanted to be involved in this book to help other people going through the same experiences of gambling addiction. He says 'If this book was out there when I was gambling it could have saved me getting deeper and deeper into some serious situations.'

Gambling affected Guy in many ways.

1: Social

Guy tended to gamble alone and not mix with other people. He kept himself to himself and didn't mention his gambling problems apart from talking about big wins when he got them. He felt people in the bookies and casino knew him and that became part of his social network and his identity.

2: Financial

Guy didn't own his own property, had no savings and no plans for the future (his outlook was very short term). He was hoping to get lucky and win his way to being wealthy. Guy had no problem racking up credit cards to gain quick access to money in order to allow him to gamble. He fell into debts of around £40,000 unsecured but probably spent in excess of £100,000.

3: Psychological

Guy was often depressed and quite frustrated, as if he was working for nothing. Sometimes Guy would have work an entire month to catch up on last month's losses. He spent a lot of time chasing losses and trying to avoid going into the betting shop. This avoidance vs approach behaviour is psychologically stressful. He felt quite stressed internally, especially after losing a lot of money.

4: Work

Guy worked to fund his playing habits. He didn't enjoy his work but did superficially if he won a lot of money. Once he'd spent the winnings this tended to be quite short lived. Sometimes he cancelled work clients to pop down to the bookies to play roulette. He would even cancel a full day's work to spend time in the casino.

Have you got a gambling problem?

1: Are you spending most of your time thinking about gambling?
2: Are you spending large amounts of money gambling?
3: Have you tried but been unsuccessful in stopping gambling in the past?
4: Do you feel angry or irritable if you try and stop?
5: Do you feel that you gamble to escape life's problems?
6: Do you often chase your losses?
7: Would you lie to friends about your gambling habits?
8: Have you ever stolen money to fund your gambling?
9: Does your gambling impact on your home life or work?
10: Do you ask friends to lend you money if you've lost?

One Yes answer: = slight problem. Seek help before it gets any worse.

Three Yes answers: = you're a problem gambler. Consider getting help, especially if you feel out of control.

Five Yes answers: = highly likely to be a pathological gambler. Seek immediate help (See help section)

Different ways gamblers may lose control

1. Not thinking about their responsibilities
2. Escape from feeling depressed
3. Boredom at home, work, or in relationships
4. Drinking or taking drugs
5. Feeling angry
6. A personal history of gambling
7. Unable to control gambling
8. Family members had gambling problems

I would advise anyone who is out of control with gambling to stop completely, especially if you struggle to control your urges or impulses.

The negative impact of having a gambling problem on Guy's life

Gambling, like many other addictions can impact on a person's life in a variety of different ways. Guy had panic attacks and suicidal thoughts. He also recalled how it had led to a breakdown of a 10 year relationship, going into voluntary bankruptcy and losing his job. These are serious consequences of having a gambling problem.

Guy's anxiety disorder tended to get worse when he was losing. Guy recalled that sometimes his anxiety levels were so high that he felt panicky and had to leave the shop. Sometimes he would bet everything on one roulette spin just so he could leave the shop. One thing that Guy did was to list all the negatives of the gambling shop. He'd dwell on those rather than what he found exciting. For example, wasting all his hard earned money, making him feel stressed or broke.

How to quit

Gambling like any other addiction is very difficult to stop. It requires self-control, discipline and a change of life style. Many gamblers, even when they are down and out, still believe they can win big. This thought process can hinder the process of stopping as they never know when to stop. This creates a vicious cycle. The options they then have are either to get into more debt, steal or sell things they own.

When Guy stopped gambling he gave this advice:

1: **Time** - don't allow yourself spare time or moments of boredom.

2: **Money** - don't give yourself access to money. Leave cards at home or cut them up.

*3: **Location*** - change your location away from betting shops.

*4: **Self-exclude*** - from the shops in the local area or when you're on holiday.

*5: **Block*** - gambling websites using software.

Tips to help you stop gambling

1: MONEY

Limit your access to money and how much you have available. Leave any cash cards at home and don't drive back home to get them if you're losing. It's all about discipline. If you feel you lack self-control be even harder on yourself. When you get paid at work, settle all the important bills first - gas, mortgage and electricity. Don't take loans out to gamble or withdraw money from credit cards. This will only add to your debts and will eventually need to be repaid. Cut your credits cards up and then close the accounts. You have to be tough on yourself and not allow yourself easy access to cash. Several trips back and forth to a nearby cash machine and you'll soon reach your daily limit on withdrawals.

Gambling is not a get rich quick scheme. Don't view it as a way to make lots of money. If you have any savings, don't gamble them away. Be prepared to lose. Winning is never guaranteed. Most gamblers lose more than they win.

2: TIME

Keep busy. Don't leave large gaps in your day where you can pop to the bookies for an hour or two. Limit your access to betting shops - once a week, at the most. It's easy to feel bored and want to fill that time with some excitement. However, you will more than likely rack up more losses and end up chasing them. Try to spend more time with your family or friends to avoid being alone and bored. You could join a local sports club to get the same buzz from winning. Sometimes it may help you to talk about your urges before you set off to the bookies or the casino. This may help you think about things before you act compulsively.

3: LOCATION

If your drive to work or to a friend means passing the betting shop, change your route. You won't be tempted to pull over, go in and spend money. Changing a route is usually such a simple but effective method to avoid temptation, like not taking your bank cards out or limiting your free time. Dealing with these three factors really helps a pathological gambler cope with their urges.

Fig 4. Three contributing factors that sustain or break a gambling habit

Chapter 6

Explanations

Genetics

The biological explanation for gambling addiction mainly focuses on genetics and neurochemical factors. Pathological gambling tends to be a progressive addiction which is characterised by a pre-occupation with gambling, wanting to bet more and more and, of course, chasing losses. DSM 5 offers standard criteria for the classification of mental disorders. It looks at the three following areas:

1: The person shows a loss of control of their gambling behaviour.
2: The person shows increased frequency in gambling.
3: The person gambles despite any negative consequences.

How gamblers start

Genetic Explanation

The role of our genes can play a very important part in our gambling behaviour. According to research, gambling tends to run in families. A twin study carried out by Shah (2005) found supporting evidence for a genetic link in men that are gamblers. Further research by Black (2006) found that first degree relatives of pathological gamblers were more at risk of suffering from pathological gambling compared to more distant relatives.

This explanation is not the full picture. The environment also plays a part in any addiction. One model known as the diathesis stress model argues that it's an interaction between stress and the environment which is a key factor in becoming a gambler. This basically means that if a person has a predisposition to being a gambler then the environmental factors could trigger the gene to become active.

One such environmental factor could be access to gambling facilities or incentives to gamble (free bets). There are however some differences between the type of gambling addiction and the onset of being a pathological gambler. For example, online gambling addiction seems to take about 1 year to develop. Betting shop gambling taking about 3.5 years (Breen and Zimmerman, 2001).

Further supporting evidence suggests there two distinct types of gamblers 1: The café gambler 2: The race track gambler. The racetrack gambler bets due to the arousal produced by the game (playing active games). The café gambler plays passive games to avoid boredom (Bonnaire, 2006).

Cognitive Explanation

This explanations looks at how people use gambling to treat psychological symptoms. This would be an activity that lets the gambler feel benefits. For example, a pathological gambler may have an issue with depression or anxiety and use gambling as a means of coping. This doesn't mean that gambling reduces anxiety or depression (it may make these worse) but that the gambler may think they are helping. This is known as the self-medicating model. Research into this carried out by Li (2008) found that gamblers who gamble to escape pain are more likely to have other substance problems like alcohol or drugs. Of course the link between depression and gambling is only a correlation and not causation.

Learning Theory

Skinner's learning theory is based on the principles of behaviourism known as operant condition. Behaviourism assumes that all our behaviours are learnt and therefore can be unlearnt. Any behaviour that is rewarded is more likely to be repeated and any behaviour that is punished is less likely to be repeated. Thus the gambler would receive rewards when they win (such as physiological) or psychological and social rewards.

Gambling pay-outs tend to be intermittent which Skinner called intermittent schedules. When playing roulette you may win on 1 spin out of 7 but no one knows when it will pay out. If this is combined with social support when winning and psychological 'near misses' then it's probably enough to keep the person gambling. As seen earlier with Guy, he had a near miss on the 49s draw when his numbers came up and he didn't buy a ticket.

How is gambling maintained?

Genetic explanation

The argument in terms of maintaining gambling behaviour and biology comes from the pituitary-adrenal response. It is thought that the pathological gambler has an underactive pituitary adrenal response to gambling stimuli.

One research study by Paris (2010) looked at the levels of cortisol in both pathological gamblers and recreational gamblers. The participants watched their favourite method of gambling compared to a neutral activity such as a roller coaster ride. The researchers found that recreational gamblers had significantly higher levels of cortisol after watching both types of stimuli, whereas the pathological gamblers showed no cortisol increase in their salivary responses. It could be argued that pathological gamblers are high sensation seekers who have a lower perception or appreciation of risk compared to recreational gamblers (Zuckerman, 1979).

Cognitive explanation

One factor that keeps a gambler going back is irrational beliefs and cognitive distortions. The classic gamblers' fallacy suggests a gambler thinks a completely random event like a spin on a roulette wheel can be influenced by recent events. This was evident with Guy. He thought that number patterns on previous roulette spins predicted or increased his chances of picking the next number.

Another explanation is known as superstitious behaviour that the gambler thinks can make an impact on the game. Guy would turn in a semi-circle after placing bets. This, he thought, could influence the machines' outcome and he could then beat the machine or the system. This type of thinking normally comes from some form of winning in the past associated with the current behaviour. Therefore, winning is linked to the gambler's skill. Losing is just plain old bad luck.

Learning theory

Gamblers are not used to winning every time they place a bet. They get accustomed to long periods of losses. This does not deter the gambler. They learn to expect a win to come in eventually.

This intermittent reinforcement explains why they keep doing it. Another factor in gambling behaviour comes from social approval - how family members who also gamble may actually approve of gambling. This would act as positive reinforcement and the gambler would carry on with his or her addictive behaviour. The gambler would also take on the identity of a gambler and live up to the social label (self-fulfilling prophecy).

Why would a gambler relapse?

Genetic explanation

Most pathological gamblers are high sensation seekers and need excitement and stimulation. They typically have a boredom tolerance problem. This would contribute to their repetitive gambling problems. Research found that poor tolerance for boredom can contribute to being a pathological gambler. There is of course another explanation such as the cognitive or the learning theory to explain gambling. It is in their genetic makeup.

Cognitive explanation

Most pathological gamblers will tell you about their wins but not their losses. This is the recall bias or the 'just world' hypothesis. The pathological gambler has a memory bias for overestimating their wins and underestimating their losses (Blanco, 2000). Guy, for example, might have had a string of losses. Rather than being put off from gambling he would think he's due a big pay out because he'd invested money into the machines. Gamblers often believe they deserve to win. This type of thinking explains why the pathological gambler keeps gambling despite severe losses.

Learning theory

When pathological gamblers try to quit gambling they usually find it extremely difficult and be in a position of relapse. Another part of learning theory or behaviourism is known as classical conditioning. This is where there are conditional cues in the environment such as sounds, lights or other gamblers. These act as a trigger to the gambler. This could include TV adverts for online casinos, a drive past the betting shop or even thinking about possible wins. If the pathological gambler is exposed to any of these then they are at a risk of relapse.

Some gamblers will use what's called approach/avoidance strategies when thinking about gambling. This is the struggle they have between the urge to keep gambling and the desire to quit. It creates inner turmoil for the addict. The learning theory doesn't tend to take into account any cognitive processes but the social learning theory does. This theory suggests that there is a cognitive process between stimulus and response. For example, the gambler drives past the betting shop (the stimuli) then thinks about whether or not to go in before acting.

Applying some of the above to real life:

Understanding gambling addiction with operant conditioning and biology.

If you're a gambler the chance to win big from a small stake is appealing. In the UK there are about 28 million people who have participated in gambling over the past year (Health survey for England, 2012). This equates to 68% of men and 61% of women who gambled during this period.

The sounds of a win, seeing the money rack up on the screen or coins dropping into the tray all offer a sense of reward.

The problem for the gambler is that the reward they are seeking is not from every bet. In order to feel pleasure they have to keep betting until they win again. This is what B.F. Skinner called the schedule of reinforcement. Therefore the win acts as a reward which reinforces the gambler's behaviour. They are unwittingly being conditioned to gamble.

There is also a sense that winning more is necessary to get the same feeling that you got initially. It is like a drug. You need to take more to get the same effect or buzz. Guy told me about how winning £200 felt really good. Nowadays, however, he needs to win £3000 - 4000 to feel it's worthwhile.

When looking at neurology in gambling, there's a similarity to taking any other addictive drug. Gambling results in dopamine levels being increased in the reward regions of the brain, which includes near misses and actual pay-outs. The challenge is that the gambler needs more and more each time to get the same feeling. This means spending more money, taking bigger risks and wanting to win more and more money.

Chapter 7

Treatment

The advice below is courtesy of The Counselling Directory who can be contacted at: www.counsellingdirectory.org.uk

CBT (Cognitive Behavioural Therapy) Treatment for gambling addiction

Treatment for gambling addiction is centred mainly on counselling (talking therapies) such as cognitive behavioural therapy. This can help people to understand their addiction and learn new, sustainable ways of managing their urge to gamble. Medication can also be provided for people whose gambling problem is linked to mental health issues such as depression, while additional treatment will be required to tackle substance abuse if this is a further concern.

Significantly, very few cases of gambling addiction are isolated - many people with a gambling problem also may have a co-occurring condition (anxiety/depression). Health professionals providing treatment will therefore look to address a range of issues that may be underlying a person's compulsion to misuse substances and gamble.

Each person will have their own unique gambling problem. Treatment is therefore tailored to ensure it meets the individual needs of each client. A key aspect of counselling is finding what triggers the addiction. What compels people to compulsively gamble even when they are aware of the negative consequences?

Understanding the reason behind gambling urges - whether it's to numb unpleasant feelings, solve money problems, escape stress or simply boredom or loneliness - can help people focus on healthier and more constructive ways of coping, without having to resort to gambling. Cognitive behavioural therapy is ultimately designed to guide clients through a process of change - helping them to rewire their thoughts and beliefs and encouraging them to aspire towards a future free from their addiction.

Overcoming a gambling addiction can be a tough process. Extra* support may be needed following counselling to ensure the recovery is maintained. Treatment however - particularly cognitive behavioural therapy - has proved highly successful in providing people with alternative means of dealing with their problems. It equips them with the necessary tools and support to reframe thoughts and behaviours for the long-term.

What should I be looking for in a counsellor or psychotherapist?

Whilst there are currently no official rules and regulations in position to stipulate what level of training and experience a counsellor dealing with gambling addiction needs, we do recommend that you check that your therapist is experienced in the area for which you are seeking help.

There are several accredited courses, qualifications and workshops available to counsellors that can improve their knowledge of a particular area. For peace of mind you may wish to check if they have had further training in matters of addiction.

For psychological treatment NHS Choices suggest cognitive behavioural therapy (CBT) to be used as tool to break the habit of addiction.

What is cognitive behavioural therapy?

Cognitive behavioural therapy - also known as CBT - combines two different approaches for a practical and solution-focused therapy. The therapy is very active by nature and requires you to take a proactive role within the treatment; this includes carrying out homework assignments outside your sessions.

The premise behind CBT is that our thoughts and behaviours have an effect on each other. By changing the way we think and behave - we can ultimately alter our feelings about life. The therapy examines learnt behaviours and negative thought patterns in order to alter them in a positive way.

Unlike some other therapies, CBT is rooted in the present and looks ahead to the future. While past events and experiences are considered during the therapy, the focus is more on current issues and dilemmas. The therapy takes its cue from two different psychological approaches:

1. Cognitive approach

Cognitive processes refer to our thoughts - including ideas, beliefs and attitudes. The cognitive element of CBT looks at the way our thoughts can trigger or fuel certain feelings and behaviours. Within CBT your therapist will help you understand any negative thought patterns you may have, how they affect you and, more importantly, what you can do to change them.

2. Behavioural approach

Behavioural therapy notes that behaviour is often learned and can therefore be unlearned. It looks at harmful or maladaptive behaviours and helps you to understand why they occur and what you can do to alter them.

CBT looks at how both cognitive and behavioural processes affect one another, and aims to help you get out of negative cycles. The emphasis on behavioural or cognitive approaches will depend on the nature of the issue you are facing - for example, if you are suffering from depression or anxiety, the emphasis may be more so on the cognitive approach, whereas if you have a condition that causes unhelpful behaviour (such as obsessive compulsive disorder), the emphasis is likely to be on the behavioural approach.

What happens in a CBT session?

Cognitive behavioural therapy can be one-to-one or as part of group therapy. Whichever format you choose, the relationship you'll have with your therapist should be a collaborative one. This means that you will take an active involvement in the therapy and will have a say in the way your sessions progress. Issues will be discussed in confidence and without judgement to help you view them in a more pragmatic light.

The therapy itself tends to last somewhere between six weeks and six months, depending on the nature of the concern being explored. Usually you will attend one session a week, with each session lasting around 50 minutes to an hour. At the start of your therapy you will meet your therapist and discuss what has brought you to therapy. At this point you will have the opportunity to outline what you would like to gain from CBT and set yourself some goals.

Together with your therapist you will then work on the content and structure of your sessions. Your therapist may set you certain tasks to do as homework. You will be able to talk about how you found these tasks during your weekly session. As your therapy progresses you will take a more prominent role in the content and structure of sessions. The idea is that by the end of your course of treatment, you should feel able to carry on the work alone.

Who could benefit from CBT?

This type of therapy is particularly helpful for those with specific issues as it is very practical (rather than insight-based) and looks at solutions. For this reason the therapy works well for those who:

- suffer from depression and/or anxiety
- have an eating disorder
- suffer from post-traumatic stress disorder (PTSD)
- have an addiction
- want to change their behaviour
- have anger issues
- suffer from insomnia
- have a phobia
- suffer from obsessive-compulsive behaviour.

In some cases CBT is used for those with long-standing health problems such as chronic pain or irritable bowel syndrome (IBS). While the therapy cannot cure such physical ailments, it can help people cope emotionally with their condition and lower stress levels. There is also up and coming interest in the use of CBT alongside medication to help those who suffer from hallucinations and delusions.

How does CBT work?

Cognitive behavioural therapy looks to help you make sense of what can feel like an overwhelming problem by breaking it down into more manageable parts. These smaller parts are your thoughts, feelings, actions and even physical sensations. These elements are interconnected and can often trap you in a negative spiral. For example, if your marriage or relationship has come to an end, you may think you have failed and that you are not capable of being in a functional relationship. These thoughts can lead to you feeling lonely, depressed and low on energy. When you feel like this, you are unlikely to want to socialise or go out and meet new people. This negative spiral can then trap you into feeling alone and unhappy.

Rather than accepting these negative thought patterns, CBT aims to show you other ways of reacting so you can break out of negative cycles. Instead of thinking that you are a failure when a relationship ends, you can choose to learn from your mistakes and move on, feeling optimistic about the future. This new way of thinking may then result in you feeling more energetic and social, helping you to meet new people and one day start a new relationship.

This is a simplified example, but it does illustrate how easy it is to get trapped in negative cycles, and how changing the way you think and behave can affect you in a significant way. In CBT you will learn to recognise your thoughts, behaviours and feelings while learning other, potentially more helpful ways of thinking and behaving.

Why do we think negatively?

Negative thinking patterns often stem from childhood and quickly become an automatic reaction. An example of this would be if you parents didn't show you much affection until you did well at school. This may cause you to associate not doing well with rejection. When you grow up, this can lead to problems when faced with failure - your automatic reaction to not succeeding may be that others will reject you.

CBT would aim to explain why you think in this way and help you to consider new ways of thinking. Through a variety of assignments and 'experiments' you will be able to face your fears of failure head on with little consequence. Testing out new ways of thinking may show you more helpful and productive ways of viewing things - and then it is just a case of practising until it becomes second nature.

Some common gamblers' thoughts and how to restructure them:

1. 'I think my lucky numbers will come up today, I'd better go and put a bet on.'

   Change to: 'The odds of my numbers coming up today are minimal, it's better to stay away and do something more productive.'

2. 'I'll just pop back to the cash point and get my last £100.'

   Change to: 'I've now reached my gambling limit. Going back to the cash point will just put me further behind. It's better to leave now.'

3. 'This fruity has been pumped and I'm the one who's invested in it. It owes me.'

Change to: 'This is not a human. It's a computer and the odds are fixed. I have set my limit and after that I'll walk away. The machine doesn't recognise me or anyone else.'

4. If you have a thought such as: 'I'm feeling lucky today, I might hit the big win.'

Change to: 'My feelings can't influence the machines, I'm better off trying to keep busy, saving the money. If I lost I would have nothing left and it would cause me even more stress.'

If you practise changing your thinking patterns it can prevent you from not giving in to the urges and impulse that problem gamblers have. This is the feeling that you must go in because if you don't you may miss out on the big win. In reality, there's a very slim chance of winning big in the betting shops. The challenge is to resist the thought that if on that day your numbers did come up then you would be kicking yourself for not putting the bet on.

This happened to Guy. One day he was going to put £15 on 2, 5, 7 on the 49s draw. He didn't, but his numbers came up. In his mind he had lost out on over £10,000. The result is that he doesn't want to miss out again. So he ended up going back in again, placing higher bets trying to win back the £10,000 he felt he had lost.

The way he broke out of this was to think that he could be spending £100s per week chasing the dream win that may never come and he would actually be worse off. If he changed his life and general unhappiness, he would not have the same drive to gamble. He would be less bored, more at peace with himself and have less time on his hands.

Learning coping skills

As well as identifying negative thought patterns, cognitive behavioural therapy can teach you the skills you need to help you deal with different problems. The hope is that once you are armed with these coping skills, you will be able to turn to them in the future when you have finished therapy.

Examples of the types of coping skills you may learn include:

- If you have a phobia or suffer from anxiety, you may discover through therapy that avoiding situations can actually increase your fears. Confronting fears in a gradual and manageable way can help you gain faith in your ability to cope.
- If you suffer from depression, your therapist may ask you to note down your thoughts so you can explore them more realistically. This can help you gain perspective and break the negative cycle.
- If you find it difficult to relate to others, you may learn to consider your assumptions about other people's motivations rather than immediately thinking the worst.

The pros and cons of CBT

Just like all psychological therapies, CBT may not be suitable for everyone. Speaking to a professional, such as a doctor or counsellor, will help you decide which therapy type is right for you and which approaches to consider. The following should help you when you are making your decision.

Pros:

- CBT has been shown to be as effective as medication in treating many mental health conditions, including depression.
- As CBT is highly structured, it can be provided in a variety of formats, including group therapy and self-help.
- The skills you learn in CBT can be incorporated into everyday life to help you cope better after your therapy is finished.
- CBT can be completed in a relatively short time frame when compared with other talk therapies.

Cons:

- In order to benefit from the therapy, you need to fully commit yourself to the process - including homework.
- As CBT is solution-focused, it works best with specific concerns rather than more complex mental health issues.
- CBT addresses current problems and some critics argue that it doesn't explore possible underlying causes fully.
- As CBT is generally time-limited, those with complex issues may benefit from longer-term treatments.

Is CBT effective?

So far, clinical trials have shown cognitive behavioural therapy to be incredibly helpful for a range of mental health concerns. In some cases the therapy is proven to be just as effective as drug therapies, especially in the treatment of depression and anxiety. Because of this, the National Institute of Health and Care Excellence (NICE) now recommends CBT to those with common mental health concerns such as depression and anxiety.

The results aren't clear about whether or not the therapy is as effective (or more effective) than other forms of talking therapy, other forms of therapy are also effective; the key is finding the right therapy type for you.

Is CBT right for me?

Now that you know a little more about the therapy, you should be in a better position to decide whether or not CBT is right for you. The therapy will be more useful to those who relate to the ideas behind it, including the solution-focused approach, the ideas about behaviour/thinking patterns and the importance of completing out of session homework.

Being committed and doing the assignments set for you is an integral part of CBT. While the sessions offer support and space to explore your concerns, it is the work you do outside of your sessions that is likely to have the most impact. By staying focused and completing assignments you will help yourself progress quicker and will develop a stronger sense of self-confidence.

CBT has been found to be effective in reducing how often a person gambles, how much they lose and rates of relapse. A pathological gambler thinks completely differently to a non-gambler or recreational gambler. The pathological gambler will have certain beliefs that other people don't have. For example they may believe that 1: They are more likely to win than the odds predict. 2: They can influence the machines and that the machines have a mind and feelings 3: They have special skills and can predict what numbers on a roulette wheel will come up 4: They can win back their losses plus more as they have invested in the machine. The machine should be due to pay out.

CBT really helps the pathological gambler to see how their thinking is irrational and not productive. It helps them alter their thought processes, restructure their thinking and change their negative beliefs. CBT is quite expensive if you have it privately. You could first speak to your GP about your gambling problems and see if any help is available.

[CBT advice courtesy of www.counsellingdirectory.org.uk]

(adapted by Stephen Renwick)

Chapter 8

The following advice is courtesy from The Royal College of Psychiatry and The Gambling Concern Charity (Dr Henrietta Bowden-Jones).

Dr Henrietta Bowden-Jones, Consultant psychiatrist at CNWL NHS Trust and Founder and Director of the National Problem Gambling Clinic offers some excellent advice on problem gambling. Dr Bowden-Jones is a psychiatrist with many years' experience dealing with problem gamblers and addicts. Below is some advice from the patient information leaflet she co-wrote with Dr Sanju George for the Royal College of Psychiatrists.

Problem gambling

What is problem gambling?

This is defined as gambling that disrupts or damages personal, family or recreational pursuits.

How common is problem gambling?

Many of us like to place the odd bet or play the lottery - but it's only a problem for about 9 people in every 1000. However, a further 70 people out of every 1000 gamble at risky levels that can become a problem in the future.

Who is most likely to get this problem?

Across the world it seems to be common:

- Men – but this might just be because women gamble less than men.
- Teenagers and young adults - but problems of this sort can start at any age. Children as young as 7 may find it difficult to control the amount of time they spend on computer games. Older people may have too much time on their hands.
- If someone else in your family - particularly one of your parents - is a problem gambler. This may be partly due to genes but can be learnt – by seeing a parent gamble or being taught to gamble by them.
- In people who work in casinos, betting shops or amusement arcades.

In certain types of gambling:

- Video poker
- Dice games
- Playing sports for money
- High-risk stocks
- Roulette
- Internet gambling
- If you drink heavily or use illegal drugs.

If you have depression, anxiety or bipolar disorder (manic depression).

Is it a problem for me?

Answer 'yes' or 'no' to each of these 10 questions:

- Do I spend a lot of time thinking about gambling?
- Am I spending larger amounts of money on my gambling?
- Have I tried to cut down or stop gambling - but not been able to?
- Do I get restless or irritable if I try to cut down my gambling?
- Do I gamble to escape from life's difficulties or to cheer myself up?
- Do I carry on playing after losing money - to try and win it back?
- Have I lied to other people about how much time or money I spend gambling?
- Have I ever stolen money to fund my gambling?
- Has my gambling affected my relationships or my job?
- Do I get other people to lend me money when I have lost?

If you have answered 'yes'

- **Just once** - May be a problem - this one thing may be enough of a problem to need help.
- **Three times** - Problem gambling - your gambling probably feels out of control - think about getting help.
- **Five or more times** - Pathological gambling - you're gambling is probably affecting every part of your life - get help.

How do you lose control of your gambling?

You may gamble:

- to forget about responsibilities

- to feel better when you feel depressed or sad
- to fill your time when bored (especially if not working)
- when you drink or use drugs
- when you get angry with others - or yourself

Or, you may have:

- started gambling early – some people start as young as 7 or 8
- never been able to control your gambling
- one or both parents who are problem gamblers

Potential harms associated with problem gambling

Problem gamblers are more likely than other people to experience the following harms:

- Financial harms: overdue utility bills; borrowing from family friends and loan sharks; debts; pawning or selling possessions; eviction or repossession; defaults; committing illegal acts like fraud, theft, embezzlement to finance gambling; bankruptcy; etc...
- Family harms: preoccupied with gambling so normal family life becomes difficult; increased arguments over money and debts; emotional and physical abuse, neglect and violence towards spouse/partner and/or children; relationship problems and separation/divorce.
- Health harms: low self-esteem; stress-related disorders; anxious, worried or mood swings; poor sleep and appetite; substance misuse; depression, suicidal ideas and attempts; etc...

- School/college/work harms: poor school, college or work performance; increased absenteeism; expulsion or dismissal.

Should I stop gambling or try to control it?

The first thing is to decide to get help - you can then work out whether you are ready to stop or just want to control your gambling better. Many people just want to control their gambling, but then decide to stop completely.

Steps to reduce gambling - helping yourself

Although there is no substitute for professional help, here are some simple and practical measures to reduce gambling:

1. Limit the amount of money you spend gambling

- Set a limit from the start on how much you are willing to spend on gambling in a session or in a week. Stick to it!
- Leave credit/cash cards at home when you go out to gamble.
- If you use a betting account, ask them to place a limit on it - say £50 - this works for online casinos too!
- On pay day, aim to pay all your priority debts first (mortgage, rent, council tax, food, etc...)

2. Reduce the amount of time and days that you gamble

- Set yourself a limit on how many times a week you will gamble - be specific and name the days.
- Avoid those "I'll just have a quick go" scenarios.

- You can set your alarm on your watch or phone to remind you - even your PC will have a calendar reminder alert you can use.

3. Don't view gambling as a way of making money

- Always remember that you are buying entertainment.
- Always be prepared to lose - if you win, know that it will happen by chance.
- Never spend your savings or investments on gambling.
- Ask friends and family not to lend you money if you ask them.

4. Spend time doing other activities

- Spend more time with family or friends.
- Take up a new hobby or interest or revisit one that you enjoyed before gambling took over.
- Join a social group or organise events with friends who don't gamble.
- Talk to other about your worries or concerns rather than 'bottling' them up.

Where can I get help?

All of the following provide free support to help you cut down or stop gambling:

NHS: The CNWL National Problem Gambling Clinic in London has doctors, nurses, therapists, psychologists, debt counsellors and family therapists with special experience in helping problem gamblers.

Gamcare - runs the national Helpline and its online equivalent, the NetLine, to offer help and support for people with a gambling problem, their family and friends. GamCare also provides face-to-face online counselling in many parts of the UK.

The Gordon Moody Association - a charity which provides treatment and housing for problem gamblers.

The 12 step meetings of Gamblers Anonymous.

Gamanon: groups for relatives of problem gamblers.

What sort of help is there?

Cognitive Behavioural Therapy (CBT)
Research has shown that CBT can:

- reduce the number of days a person gambles
- reduce the amount of money they lose
- help a gambler to stay away from gambling once they have stopped.

How does CBT work? If you are a problem gambler, you will think differently from other people about your betting. You will tend to believe that:

- you are more likely to win than you would expect by chance;
- in a game with random numbers, like roulette, certain numbers are more likely to come up than others;
- winning twice in a row means that you are on a 'winning streak' – so you bet larger and larger sums;

- you are more likely to win at a game of chance if you are familiar with it;
- certain rituals can bring you luck;
- having lost, you can somehow win back your losses by gambling more.

CBT is given in around 10 one-hour sessions. The sessions focus on these ways of thinking, but also on how you feel and behave when you want to bet or when you are gambling. CBT helps you to work out more helpful ways of thinking and behaving. A diary helps you to keep track of your improvement. In the months following treatment, follow-up CBT sessions in a group seem to help people stay away from gambling longer.

How does CBT compare with other treatments?

We don't know yet - there have not been enough large studies to be clear about this.

Medication

No medication is licensed for the treatment of problem gambling in the UK, but antidepressants can be prescribed to help with low mood.

Series Editor: Dr Philip Timms

Original Authors:

1. Dr Henrietta Bowden – Jones, National Problem Gambling Clinic & Imperial College, London

2. Dr Sanju George, Birmingham and Solihull Mental Health NHS Foundation Trust

With thanks to:

Dr Henrietta Bowden-Jones

FRCPsych, BA(Hons), DOccMed, MD(Imperial)

Director and Lead Clinician, National Problem Gambling Clinic, London.

CNWL NHS Foundation Trust

Royal College of Psychiatrists Spokesperson on Behavioural Addictions.

Chapter 9

FINAL THOUGHTS FROM GUY

FREE YOURSELF FROM GAMBLING

Guy said that now he has quit gambling for good he has a lot of time on his hands. It's a good idea to keep busy, maybe rekindle an old hobby or passion. Playing sports is a great way to get a natural high and will also help keep you fit. Rather than spending hundreds of pounds in the bookies, as a reward for not gambling, go and treat yourself to a nice meal.

Spend more time with your family and friends. Take up activities together rather than spending time alone gambling. Use your money wisely, invest in your future, buy property or develop a business. Learn the lessons from being a gambling addict and swear never to gamble again. Take a clean break and a fresh start. Be kind to yourself and focus on your qualities rather than on what you're lacking. See how less stressed you feel now you're not gambling and chasing any losses. There's a lot less anxiety inside you now. You will probably even sleep better as you won't be stressing out over money that you've lost.

Overall, alter your lifestyle radically. Change your thoughts and vision for the future. Emphasise other ways of spending your time. Enjoy a life free from gambling. You can break the pattern of your addiction if you are willing to take things day by day and use baby steps. Finally, don't be afraid of asking for help, you are not alone and there are professionals such as Dr Henrietta Bowden-Jones who can help you stop gambling.

For Advice On Where to Turn if You Need Help

NHS Choices
Gambling Addiction
Read about gambling addiction, its effects and treatment options, and where to get help.
Royal College of Psychiatrists Leaflet
www.rcpsych.ac.uk/mentalhealthinfo

Gamcare
Helpline: 0808 8020 133
gamcare.org.uk
A confidential counselling, advice and information service for people affected by a gambling dependency, including family and friends of compulsive gamblers.

Gamblers Anonymous (UK)
Helplines: See contact page for regional phone numbers
gamblersanonymous.org.uk
Provides information about a fellowship of men and women who have joined together to do something about their own gambling problem.
Helpline 08700 50 88 80 24 hours a day every day National rate
www.gamanon.org.uk

For anyone affected by someone else's gambling
National Debt line Helpline: 0808 808 4000
nationaldebtline.co.uk

<u>National Problem Gambling</u>
Address: Crowther Market, 282 North End Road, London SW6 1NH
Phone: 02073817722
Fax: 020 7381 7723
gambling.cnwl@nhs.net

<u>Gambling Concern Charity</u>
www.justgiving.com/gambling-concern

References

Books

A Clinician's Guide to Working with Problem Gamblers Paperback (2015) by Henrietta Bowden-Jones (Editor), Sanju George (Editor).

Overcoming Problem Gambling: A Guide for Problem and Compulsive Gamblers (Overcoming Common Problems) (2010) by Philip Mawer.

Psychology A2, The Complete Companion Student Book, Oxford University Press 238-245, (2012) Cardwell, M and Flanagan, C.

Pathological Gambling: Etiology, Comorbidity, and Treatment, (2013) Nancy M. Petry.

Websites

Counselling Directory

www.counsellingdirectory.org.uk [accessed 7th August, 2015]

Gambling Commission

http://www.gamblingcommission.gov.uk/pdf/british%20 gambling%20prevalence%20survey%202010%20-%20executive%20 summary.pdf [accessed 1st September 2015]

www.gov.uk

https://www.gov.uk/government/uploads/system/uploads/attachment_data/file/248922/Association_of_British_Bookmakers.pdf [accessed 1st September 2015]

The Royal College of Psychiatrists

www.rcpsych.ac.uk [accessed 7th August, 2015]

This is Money

http://www.thisismoney.co.uk/money/news/article-2973604/Brits-blowing-1-7BILLION-year-betting-machines.html [accessed 1st September 2015]

www.insidethemindofagambler.co.uk